# NORTH STAR
*the shining light that saved a life*

**Written & Designed by Matt Johnston**

ISBN: 9798340711113

Copyright © 2024 Matt Johnston

For my North Star
to the moon & back

— M —

This book is for me.

It's for you.

It's for anyone who felt alone in the dark,

helpless and lost.

You have a North Star out there.

You just have to let it find you

# THE
# STRUGGLE

Drowning

Drowning
Drowning but swimming

Drowning
Drowning but swimming
Does that even make sense?

Living a life,
wearing a mask
The mask of happiness
hiding the face of misery

Life spiralling whilst
trying to keep it on the
straight and narrow

Everything to live for
but not wanting to live

It felt like I was swimming against an unrelenting tide,
struggling for breath, pretending that everything was fine

The weight of expectations, of life itself, dragged me deeper into a sea of despair

But even in the distance, I began to notice a faint light. My **North Star**, steady and unwavering, shining quietly above the waves

# THE
## ABYSS

Is there an escape apart
from death?
Is death even an escape?

                    How do we move
                    forward from here?
                    How do I get back
                          to "normal"?

Who am I even talking to at this point?

Putting words on a page seems right but scares me because it's facing the truth

Questions echoed in my mind, dark and unsettling. It was as though I had been swallowed by the abyss, and every answer seemed out of reach.

Yet, even in the thickest fog of uncertainty, I could feel the gentle pull of something guiding me forward.

My **North Star** never asked for anything, never judged my confusion, it simply illuminated the next step.

# THE
# CONTRADICTION

Is my life just one big contradiction?

My family, my friends

They make me richer than so many people, yet why do I feel so emotionally poor?

Life felt like a paradox, filled with blessings yet weighed down by sadness. It seemed unfair to feel this way, especially when I had so much to be grateful for

But the light from my **North Star** didn't waver. It reminded me that contradictions are part of the journey, that sometimes feeling lost is how we learn to find ourselves again

# THE
# CROSSROADS

Is this the beginning of the end?
Or just the end of the beginning?

I'm a shell.

An empty shell

I guess I can either fill it and grow or just leave it there in the wasteland

I found myself standing at a crossroads, unsure of which path to take. To stay empty or to begin the long road towards growth?

But I wasn't doing it alone. My **North Star** was there, constant and steady, quietly encouraging me to fill that shell

with hope,

With purpose.

# THE
## LIGHT

And for anyone else reading this, you're not alone.

Anguish and pain is normal.

The pain, the sadness

These were not unique to me.

They are part of being human, part of the journey towards something better.

And while I couldn't see the way forward on my own, the light of my **North Star** showed me that I wasn't alone. Together, we could navigate the darkness.

# THE
## CHANGE

I'm sad.

Really, really sad.

I just want to end the darkness
and be happy again,
but I don't know how.

I hate who I've become.

It isn't me.

I don't even recognise
myself anymore.

How do I change it?

The sadness was real, and so was the desire for change. It was hard to see a way out, to recognise the person I once was beneath the layers of despair.

But my **North Star**

my constant,

my guide,

showed me that change was
not only possible

# THE
## HOPE

I may not have had
all the answers,
but I knew one thing:

                        I wasn't walking
                          this path alone.

My **North Star** was there,

as they always had been,

shining brightly and showing me the way forward.

And though the darkness still lingered, their love and guidance gave me the strength to believe that,

*I could find my way back to the light.*

To the person who took the time to read this.

Thank You.

This was my journey through the dark.

If this book has helped you, resonated with you
or made you feel anything at all,
I am eternally grateful

Printed in Great Britain
by Amazon